Effective Parenting Strategies for Navigating DMDD at Home

A Guide to Understanding, Supporting, and Empowering Your Child with Disruptive Mood Dysregulation Disorder

By

Scott Palmer

Table of Contents

INTRODUCTION

Mary had always known that her daughter, Sarah, was a little different from other children her age. As a toddler, she would often have tantrums that seemed out of proportion to the situation at hand. As Sarah grew older, these outbursts became more frequent and intense. Mary often found herself feeling overwhelmed and helpless in the face of Sarah's seemingly uncontrollable mood swings.

It wasn't until Sarah was seven years old that she was diagnosed with Disruptive Mood Dysregulation Disorder (DMDD). Mary was initially relieved to have a name for the behavior that had been causing so much stress in their home, but she quickly realized that the diagnosis was only the beginning of a long and difficult journey.

Mary and her husband, John, tried everything they could think of to help Sarah. They read books on parenting and childhood development, talked to experts, and tried various therapies and medications. Some things seemed to help a little, but nothing provided the lasting relief they were hoping for.

As Sarah's behavior continued to deteriorate, Mary found herself struggling to cope. She became increasingly isolated, as it became harder and harder to take Sarah out in public without triggering a meltdown. She found herself constantly on edge, dreading the next outburst and feeling like she was always walking on eggshells.

One day, Mary hit rock bottom. She had just gotten Sarah off to school and was sitting alone in her quiet house, feeling completely overwhelmed and defeated. She didn't know how much longer she could keep going like this. As tears streamed down her face, Mary realized that she needed help.

She reached out to a support group for parents of children with DMDD, and it was a turning point for her. For the first time, Mary found herself surrounded by people who understood what she was going through. She heard stories from other parents who had faced similar challenges and overcome them. She learned new strategies for managing Sarah's behavior and coping with her own stress and anxiety.

Slowly but surely, Mary began to regain her confidence as a parent. She started to see that there was hope for Sarah's future, and that she could make a real difference in her daughter's life. With the help of her support group, Mary began to implement new techniques for managing Sarah's behavior. She learned to identify triggers and avoid them whenever possible. She practiced de-escalation techniques to help Sarah calm down when she started to get upset. She even started a reward system to encourage positive behaviors and help Sarah feel more in control.

It wasn't easy, and there were obstacles along the way. But Mary kept pushing forward, fueled by the love and determination she felt for her daughter. As time went on, she began to see real progress. Sarah's outbursts became less frequent and less severe. Mary found herself feeling more confident and in control as a parent.

Today, Sarah is a thriving teenager. She still has her challenges, but Mary feels better equipped to handle them. She knows that there will be bumps in the road, but she also knows that they can overcome them together. Mary is grateful for the support group that helped her find her footing as a parent, and for the love and resilience that she and Sarah share. They may not have had an easy journey, but they are stronger for it, and they know that they can face whatever challenges come their way.

Disruptive Mood Dysregulation Disorder (DMDD) is a relatively new diagnosis in the world of mental health. It was added to the Diagnostic and Statistical Manual of Mental Disorders (DSM-5) in 2013, replacing the previous diagnosis of "childhood bipolar disorder." DMDD is characterized by severe and recurring rage tantrums that are out of proportion to the context and inconsistent with the child's developmental level. These outbursts must occur three or more times per week for at least 12 months, and must be present in at least two settings (such as home and school). The diagnosis cannot be made before the age of six or after the age of 18.

While DMDD is a relatively new diagnosis, it is becoming increasingly recognized and studied. According to the National Institute of Mental Health (NIMH), the prevalence of DMDD in the United States is estimated to be around 2% to 5% of children, with higher rates in clinical samples. This means that, of the approximately 74 million children under the age of 18 in the US, around 1.5 to 3.7 million may have DMDD.

DMDD appears to be more common in boys than in girls, and is often co-occurring with other mental health disorders such as ADHD, anxiety, and depression. There is some evidence to suggest that children with a family history of bipolar disorder may be more likely to develop DMDD.

The prevalence of DMDD outside of the United States is not as well-established, as it is a relatively new diagnosis and has not yet been widely studied in many countries. However, studies in other countries have suggested that DMDD may be a significant mental health concern worldwide. For example, a study of children in Singapore found that DMDD was the most common psychiatric disorder among children seeking mental health treatment.

One of the challenges of studying DMDD is that it can be difficult to distinguish from other childhood psychiatric disorders. For example, some children who are diagnosed with DMDD may actually have ADHD or bipolar disorder. This has led some experts to question whether DMDD is a distinct disorder or simply a new name for previously recognized conditions.

Despite these challenges, the recognition of DMDD as a distinct diagnosis has helped to raise awareness of the unique challenges faced by children and families affected by the disorder. Research into effective treatments for DMDD is ongoing, and there is hope that with early identification and appropriate intervention, children with DMDD can go on to lead happy and fulfilling lives.

Part I

Understanding DMDD

What is DMDD ?

Disruptive Mood Dysregulation Disorder (DMDD) is a relatively new diagnosis in the world of mental health. It is characterized by serious and recurrent temper outbursts that are out of proportion to the situation at hand, as well as inconsistent with the child's developmental level. While DMDD is becoming increasingly recognized and studied, it can be difficult to distinguish from other childhood psychiatric disorders. The recognition of DMDD as a distinct diagnosis has helped to raise awareness of the unique challenges faced by children and families affected by the disorder. With ongoing research and intervention, children with DMDD can go on to lead happy and fulfilling lives.

Symptoms and Diagnosis of DMDD

Disruptive Mood Dysregulation Disorder (DMDD) is a childhood-onset disorder characterized by severe and recurrent temper outbursts that are grossly out of proportion to the situation at hand. In this section, we will explore the symptoms of DMDD and the diagnostic criteria used to identify the disorder.

Symptoms of DMDD

The hallmark symptom of DMDD is severe and recurrent temper outbursts. These outbursts are characterized by a persistent irritable or angry mood and occur at least three times per week for a period of 12 months or more. The outbursts are typically more severe than what would be expected for the child's developmental level and can be extremely disruptive to their life.

In addition to the temper outbursts, children with DMDD may also exhibit symptoms such as:

- Frequent and severe irritability or anger outside of the temper outbursts
- Difficulty functioning in social, academic, or family settings due to their behavior
- Chronic sadness or hopelessness
- Difficulty sleeping or frequent nightmares
- Fatigue or low energy
- Difficulty concentrating or making decisions
- Feelings of worthlessness or guilt
- Recurrent thoughts of death or suicide
- It is important to note that these symptoms must be present for at least 12 months and must be present in at least two settings, such as home and school.

Diagnosis of DMDD

The diagnosis of DMDD is made using the criteria outlined in the Diagnostic and Statistical Manual of Mental Disorders, Fifth Edition (DSM-5). To be diagnosed with DMDD, a child must meet the following criteria:

- Severe temper outbursts that are grossly out of proportion to the situation, occurring three or more times per week for at least 12 months
- The temper outbursts must be inconsistent with the child's developmental level
- The temper outbursts must occur in at least two settings, such as home and school
- There must be persistent irritability or anger between the temper outbursts that is present most of the day, nearly every day
- The symptoms must be present for at least 12 months, and there must be no period of three or more consecutive months during which the child does not have the symptoms
- The symptoms must cause significant impairment in social, academic, or family functioning

It is important to note that the diagnosis of DMDD should only be made by a qualified mental health professional, such as a psychiatrist or psychologist. This is because there are other conditions that can mimic the symptoms of

DMDD, such as bipolar disorder or ADHD, and a thorough evaluation is necessary to ensure an accurate diagnosis.

In addition to a clinical evaluation, a mental health professional may also use rating scales or questionnaires to help assess the child's symptoms and determine the severity of the disorder. These measures can be helpful in tracking the child's progress over time and in monitoring their response to treatment.

Overall, the diagnosis of DMDD is based on a careful assessment of the child's symptoms and the impact they are having on their life. With early identification and appropriate treatment, children with DMDD can go on to lead happy and fulfilling lives.

How DMDD differs from other childhood disorders

Disruptive Mood Dysregulation Disorder (DMDD) is a relatively new diagnosis in the field of mental health, and it is often confused with other childhood disorders, such as bipolar disorder or oppositional defiant disorder (ODD). In this section, we will explore how DMDD differs from these and other childhood disorders.

DMDD vs. Bipolar Disorder

One of the primary differences between DMDD and bipolar disorder is the presence of manic or hypomanic episodes in bipolar disorder. Children with bipolar disorder experience periods of elevated or irritable mood, increased energy, decreased need for sleep, grandiosity, and sometimes, reckless behavior. In contrast, children with DMDD do not experience elevated mood or other symptoms of mania. Instead, they experience persistent irritability and severe temper outbursts that are out of proportion to the situation at hand.

Another difference between the two disorders is the age of onset. Bipolar disorder typically begins in adolescence or young adulthood, whereas DMDD typically begins in childhood. Additionally, children with DMDD may have a family history of depression, anxiety, or other mood disorders, whereas children with bipolar disorder may have a family history of bipolar disorder.

DMDD vs. ODD

Oppositional defiant disorder (ODD) is another childhood disorder that is often confused with DMDD. ODD is characterized by a pattern of defiant, disobedient, and hostile behavior toward authority figures. Children with ODD may argue with adults, refuse to comply with rules or requests, deliberately annoy others, and blame others for their mistakes.

While children with DMDD may exhibit some of these behaviors, the primary symptom of DMDD is severe temper outbursts. In contrast, the primary symptom of ODD is defiance and oppositionality. Children with ODD may also have a history of conduct disorder, which is characterized by more serious behavior problems, such as aggression, destruction of property, and violation of others' rights.

DMDD vs. Depression

Depression is a common mental health disorder that can also occur in children. Like DMDD, depression can cause irritability and mood swings. However, in depression, these symptoms are typically accompanied by other symptoms such as sadness, hopelessness, and loss of interest in activities that the child used to enjoy. In DMDD, the primary symptom is severe and recurrent temper outbursts that are out of proportion to the situation at hand.

DMDD vs. Anxiety

Anxiety is another common childhood disorder that can be confused with DMDD. Children with anxiety may worry excessively, have trouble sleeping, and have physical symptoms such as stomachaches or headaches. In contrast, children with DMDD do not typically experience excessive worry or physical symptoms. However, anxiety and DMDD can co-occur, meaning that a child can have both disorders at the same time.

Overall, while DMDD shares some symptoms with other childhood disorders, such as bipolar disorder, ODD, depression, and anxiety, it is a distinct diagnosis with its own set of diagnostic criteria. A thorough evaluation by a qualified mental health professional is necessary to determine whether a child's symptoms meet the criteria for DMDD or another disorder.

Causes and Risk Factors of DMDD

The causes of Disruptive Mood Dysregulation Disorder (DMDD) are not well understood, but research suggests that it may be a result of a combination of genetic, biological, and environmental factors. Here, we will explore the various causes and risk factors associated with DMDD.

Genetic Factors:

Studies have found that there may be a genetic component to DMDD. Children with a family history of mood disorders, such as depression or bipolar disorder, are more likely to develop DMDD than those without such a family history. Research suggests that certain genes may increase a child's risk for developing DMDD. However, the specific genes involved and how they interact with environmental factors to cause DMDD are not yet fully understood.

Biological Factors:

There is evidence to suggest that biological factors, such as brain chemistry, may play a role in the development of DMDD. For example, studies have found that children with DMDD have a dysregulation of the neurotransmitter serotonin, which is involved in regulating mood. Other studies have found that children with DMDD have abnormal functioning in certain regions of the brain that are involved in emotional regulation.

Environmental Factors:

Environmental factors can also contribute to the development of DMDD. For example, children who experience chronic stress or trauma, such as abuse or neglect, are more likely to develop DMDD. Additionally, children who grow up in chaotic or unstable environments may be more likely to develop DMDD.

Parenting styles can also contribute to the development of DMDD. Children who are raised in harsh, punitive, or overly permissive environments may be more likely to develop DMDD. Conversely, children who are raised in warm, supportive, and consistent environments are less likely to develop DMDD.

Risk Factors:

Several risk factors have been identified that increase a child's likelihood of developing DMDD. These risk factors include:

- Male gender: Boys are more likely to develop DMDD than girls.
- Age: DMDD typically develops between the ages of 6 and 10.
- Temperament: Children who have a difficult temperament, such as being highly sensitive or easily frustrated, may be more likely to develop DMDD.
- Co morbidities: Children with other mental health disorders, such as anxiety or ADHD, are more likely to develop DMDD.
- Family history: Children with a family history of mood disorders, such as depression or bipolar disorder, are more likely to develop DMDD.
- Environmental factors: Children who experience chronic stress or trauma, such as abuse or neglect, or who grow up in chaotic or unstable environments, are more likely to develop DMDD.

It is important to note that while these risk factors increase a child's likelihood of developing DMDD, they do not guarantee that a child will develop the disorder.

Additionally, some children with DMDD may not have any of these risk factors. A thorough evaluation by a qualified mental health professional is necessary to determine whether a child's symptoms meet the criteria for DMDD or another disorder.

Prognosis and Outcomes

Disruptive Mood Dysregulation Disorder (DMDD) is a relatively new diagnosis in the field of mental health, and research on the prognosis and outcomes of the disorder is limited. However, studies suggest that early identification and treatment can lead to improved outcomes for children with DMDD.

Prognosis

The prognosis for DMDD is generally good if the disorder is identified and treated early. Children who receive treatment for DMDD can experience a reduction in their symptoms and an improvement in their overall functioning. However, if left untreated, DMDD can lead to a range of negative outcomes, including academic and social problems, substance abuse, and other mental health disorders.

Outcomes

The outcomes of DMDD can vary depending on a range of factors, including the severity of the symptoms, the age at which the disorder is identified and treated, and the effectiveness of the treatment. Some of the potential outcomes of DMDD include:

Academic problems

Children with DMDD may have difficulty concentrating, completing tasks, and following directions, which can lead to academic problems. They may struggle in school and have a higher risk of repeating grades or dropping out.

Social problems

Children with DMDD may have difficulty getting along with peers and may be more likely to engage in aggressive or violent behavior. They may have trouble forming and maintaining relationships, which can lead to social isolation and loneliness.

Substance abuse

Studies have shown that children with DMDD are at increased risk of developing substance abuse problems later in life. This may be because they use drugs or alcohol as a way to cope with their symptoms.

Other mental health disorders

Children with DMDD are at increased risk of developing other mental health disorders, such as depression, anxiety, and conduct disorder. These disorders can further impair their functioning and lead to a range of negative outcomes.

Treatment

The treatment of DMDD typically involves a combination of medication and therapy. The most commonly used medications for DMDD are antidepressants and antipsychotics, which can help to reduce irritability and aggression. Therapy, such as cognitive-behavioral therapy (CBT), can help children learn coping skills and strategies for managing their emotions.

Early identification and treatment are crucial for improving the prognosis and outcomes of DMDD. Parents and caregivers should be aware of the symptoms of DMDD and seek professional help if they suspect that their child may be experiencing the disorder. With proper treatment, children with DMDD can go on to lead healthy and productive lives.

Part II

Creating a Supportive Environment

Parenting a child with Disruptive Mood Dysregulation Disorder (DMDD) can be challenging, but creating a supportive environment can make a significant difference in the child's well-being. Children with DMDD may struggle with regulating their emotions and behaviors, which can lead to conflict and tension in the home. However, by implementing strategies to create a supportive environment, parents can help their children learn to manage their emotions and behaviors in a healthy and constructive way. In this article, we will discuss some tips for creating a supportive environment for children with DMDD.

Strategies for creating a calm and stable home environment

Creating a calm and stable home environment is essential for children with Disruptive Mood Dysregulation Disorder

(DMDD). Children with DMDD often struggle with regulating their emotions and behaviors, which can cause conflict and tension in the home. As a result, it is essential for parents to implement strategies that can create a supportive and stable home environment. We will examine some effective parenting strategies for navigating DMDD at home and creating a calm and stable environment.

Consistency:

Consistency is critical when parenting a child with DMDD. Children with DMDD benefit from a predictable routine and a stable home environment. Parents should strive to maintain consistency in their daily routines, rules, and consequences. This can help reduce the likelihood of temper outbursts and improve the child's sense of security.

Positive Reinforcement:

Positive reinforcement is a powerful tool for shaping behavior in children with DMDD. Parents should strive to praise their child's positive behaviors and accomplishments frequently. Positive reinforcement can help motivate the child to repeat positive behaviors and help build their self-esteem.

Avoid Triggers:

Parents should be mindful of the child's triggers and avoid situations that may lead to temper outbursts. Triggers can vary from child to child, but common triggers include fatigue, hunger, and overstimulation. Parents should take steps to ensure the child is well-rested, well-fed, and not over stimulated.

Effective Communication:

Effective communication is key when parenting a child with DMDD. Parents should strive to communicate with their child in a calm and clear manner. It is important to listen to the child's feelings and concerns and validate their emotions. Parents should also use "I" statements instead of "you" statements when discussing sensitive issues. This can help reduce defensiveness and create a more supportive and collaborative environment.

Use Visual Aids:

Visual aids, such as charts and calendars, can be helpful for children with DMDD. Parents can use visual aids to help their child understand daily routines, rules, and consequences. This can help reduce anxiety and improve the child's sense of predictability and control.

Self-Care:

Parents of children with DMDD can experience high levels of stress and burnout. It is essential for parents to practice self-care and take time for themselves. This can include engaging in hobbies, exercise, and seeking support from family and friends. Taking care of oneself can help parents stay calm and focused, which can help create a more supportive and stable home environment.

The Importance of Consistency and Routine

Consistency and routine are crucial for children with Disruptive Mood Dysregulation Disorder (DMDD). Children with DMDD often struggle with regulating their emotions and behaviors, which can cause conflict and tension in the home. As a result, it is essential for parents to implement strategies that can create a supportive and stable home environment. In this section, we will discuss the importance of consistency and routine for children with DMDD and how it links to effective parenting strategies for navigating DMDD at home.

Predictability and Structure:

Consistency and routine provide children with DMDD with a sense of predictability and structure. Children with DMDD often feel overwhelmed by the unpredictability of their emotions, and having a consistent and structured environment can help them feel more in control. It also reduces anxiety and stress levels, which can lead to fewer outbursts.

Reduce Anxiety and Stress:

Anxiety and stress are common triggers for children with DMDD. By establishing a consistent routine, parents can help reduce their child's anxiety and stress levels. A routine provides the child with a sense of predictability, which can help reduce anxiety levels. It also helps the child feel more in control of their environment, which can reduce stress levels.

Learning Self-Regulation:

Children with DMDD have difficulty regulating their emotions and behaviors. By providing a consistent routine, parents can help their child learn self-regulation skills. A consistent routine helps the child understand expectations and consequences, which can help them learn to manage their emotions and behaviors more effectively.

Establishing Boundaries:

Consistency and routine help establish boundaries for children with DMDD. Children with DMDD often struggle with impulsivity, and a consistent routine can help them learn to control their impulses. It also helps parents establish boundaries and rules that are consistent and predictable, which can reduce conflicts and tension in the home.

Improve Sleep:

Sleep is crucial for children with DMDD. A consistent routine can help improve sleep patterns for children with DMDD. Children with DMDD often struggle with falling asleep and staying asleep, which can lead to fatigue and irritability. By establishing a consistent bedtime routine, parents can help their child develop healthy sleep patterns.

Tips for Reducing Stress and Anxiety in the Home

Stress and anxiety are common experiences for many people, and can be particularly prevalent in the home. Whether it's the daily grind of household responsibilities, the pressure of work, or the challenges of parenting, it's easy to feel overwhelmed and anxious in your own home. This can have a negative impact on your mental health and well-being, as well as on your relationships with family members. In this article, we will provide tips for reducing stress and anxiety in the home, and link these tips to effective parenting strategies for navigating DMDD (Disruptive Mood Dysregulation Disorder) at home.

Identify and reduce triggers

The first step in reducing stress and anxiety in the home is to identify and reduce triggers. Triggers are anything that causes you to feel stressed or anxious, and can include things like clutter, noise, or conflict. Once you have identified your triggers, you can take steps to reduce or eliminate them. For example, you may need to declutter your home, establish quiet zones, or work on conflict resolution skills with your family.

When it comes to DMDD, identifying triggers is especially important. Children with DMDD may have a low threshold for frustration and be more likely to become angry or irritable in response to stressors. As a parent, it's important to identify these triggers and work with your child to develop coping strategies.

Establish routines

Establishing routines is another effective way to reduce stress and anxiety in the home. When you have a predictable routine, you can better manage your time and responsibilities, and reduce the feeling of being overwhelmed. Routines can also provide a sense of stability and security for children, which can help to reduce their anxiety.

For children with DMDD, routines can be particularly beneficial. Children with DMDD may struggle with emotional regulation and have difficulty transitioning between activities. By establishing clear routines and sticking to them, you can help your child to feel more in control and reduce the likelihood of meltdowns or outbursts.

Practice self-care

Self-care is an essential component of managing stress and anxiety. When you take care of yourself, you are better able to deal with the challenges of everyday life. This can include activities such as exercise, meditation, getting enough sleep, and eating a nutritious diet. It's important to make self-care a priority, even when you're busy or feeling overwhelmed.

As a parent of a child with DMDD, self-care is especially important. Children with DMDD can be demanding and require a lot of emotional energy to manage. Taking time for yourself can help you to recharge and be more present and patient with your child.

Create a calm environment

Creating a calm environment can also help to reduce stress and anxiety in the home. This can include things like using soft lighting, playing calming music, and using calming scents like lavender or chamomile. It's also important to establish clear boundaries and rules, and to enforce them consistently. When everyone in the household knows what is expected of them, it can help to reduce conflicts and promote a sense of calm.

For children with DMDD, a calm environment can be particularly helpful. Children with DMDD may struggle with emotional dysregulation and be more likely to become agitated or reactive in chaotic environments. By creating a calm and predictable environment, you can help your child to feel more grounded and in control.

Practice effective communication

Effective communication is key to reducing stress and anxiety in the home. When you communicate effectively, you can resolve conflicts more easily, and promote a sense of understanding and respect among family members. This can include things like active listening, using "I" statements, and avoiding blame or criticism.

For parents of children with DMDD, effective communication is especially important. Children with DMDD may struggle with communication and have difficulty expressing their feelings in a clear and constructive way. As a parent, it's important to model effective communication and provide your child with the tools and support they need to communicate effectively. This may involve things like teaching your child to use "I" statements, encouraging them to express their feelings, and using active listening skills to understand their perspective.

In addition to these general tips for reducing stress and anxiety in the home, there are also some specific strategies that can be helpful for parents of children with DMDD:

Use positive reinforcement

Positive reinforcement is a powerful tool for promoting positive behavior in children with DMDD. Rather than focusing on punishment or negative consequences for undesirable behavior, it's important to reinforce positive behavior whenever possible. This can involve things like praise, rewards, or positive feedback.

Provide structure and routine

As mentioned earlier, providing structure and routine is important for all children, but especially for those with DMDD. By establishing clear routines and expectations, you can help your child to feel more in control and reduce the likelihood of meltdowns or outbursts. It's also important to be consistent with these routines, as inconsistency can be particularly difficult for children with DMDD.

Practice relaxation techniques

Relaxation techniques like deep breathing, progressive muscle relaxation, and guided imagery can be helpful for reducing anxiety and promoting emotional regulation in children with DMDD. These techniques can be practiced at home and can be particularly helpful during times of stress or high emotions.

How to Communicate Effectively With Your Child

Effective communication is crucial for building strong relationships with your child and for helping them navigate life's challenges. However, for parents of children with DMDD, effective communication can be particularly challenging. Children with DMDD may struggle with communication and have difficulty expressing their feelings in a clear and constructive way. As a parent, it's important to model effective communication and provide your child with the tools and support they need to communicate effectively.

Here are some tips for communicating effectively with your child, especially when dealing with DMDD:

Be an active listener

Active listening is the cornerstone of effective communication. It involves fully engaging with your child when they are speaking, paying attention to what they are saying, and responding in a way that shows you have heard and understood their message. When your child is expressing their feelings or thoughts, try to put aside any distractions or preoccupations and give them your full attention.

Use "I" statements

When expressing your personal sentiments or concerns, strive to employ "I" statements rather than "you" comments. "I" statements are less accusatory and can help to avoid defensiveness and conflict. For example, instead of saying "You always make a mess," you could say "I get frustrated when I see a messy room."

Validate their feelings

It's important to acknowledge your child's feelings and let them know that you understand and accept them. This can help them feel heard and supported, even if you don't necessarily agree with their point of view. "I can see you're really upset right now," you could add, or "It sounds like you're really angry about what happened."

Avoid criticism and judgment

Children with DMDD are often very sensitive to criticism and judgment, which can trigger defensive or angry reactions. When communicating with your child, try to avoid using negative language, criticizing or judging them, or making them feel like they are being attacked. Instead, focus on providing constructive feedback and using positive reinforcement to encourage positive behavior.

Use appropriate body language

Your body language can also play an important role in effective communication. When speaking with your child, try to maintain eye contact, use a calm and measured tone of voice, and avoid crossing your arms or showing other signs of defensiveness. Your body language should convey a sense of openness, empathy, and understanding.

When communicating with a child with DMDD, it can also be helpful to use specific strategies that are tailored to their needs. For example, you may want to try the following:

Use visual aids

Children with DMDD may benefit from visual aids, such as pictures, diagrams, or charts, to help them understand and process information. You could create a visual schedule for the day or use pictures to illustrate different emotions and their associated behaviors.

Simplify your language

Children with DMDD may have difficulty understanding complex language or abstract concepts. When communicating with your child, try to use simple, concrete language that is easy for them to understand. You may also want to break down complex tasks or instructions into smaller, more manageable steps.

Provide a calm environment

Children with DMDD may be more prone to emotional outbursts or meltdowns when they are in a high-stress environment. By creating a calm and structured environment at home, you can help your child feel more in control and reduce the likelihood of meltdowns. This may involve things like establishing a consistent routine, providing clear expectations, and avoiding loud or chaotic environments.

Part III

Positive Parenting Techniques

Positive parenting techniques are a research-based approach to raising children that emphasize nurturing, support, and mutual respect. Rather than using punitive measures, positive parenting techniques focus on understanding children's emotions and needs, and working with them to build healthy relationships and develop important life skills. For families dealing with DMDD (Disruptive Mood Dysregulation Disorder), positive parenting strategies can be particularly effective in managing challenging behaviors and improving communication. By using positive reinforcement, effective communication, and consistent discipline, parents can help their children regulate their emotions and develop a sense of security and stability at home. Positive parenting techniques are not only effective in managing difficult behaviors, but can also help families build stronger, more loving relationships that last a lifetime.

Setting Realistic Expectations and Goals

Setting realistic expectations and goals is an important aspect of effective parenting, especially when it comes to navigating DMDD at home. DMDD is a disorder that is characterized by severe and persistent irritability, frequent temper outbursts, and difficulty regulating emotions. Children with DMDD often struggle with social interactions, academic performance, and family relationships, which can put a significant strain on parents and caregivers. In order to effectively manage DMDD, it is crucial for parents to set realistic expectations and goals for their children, while also recognizing their unique strengths and limitations.

One of the first steps in setting realistic expectations and goals is to understand the nature of DMDD and how it affects children. DMDD is a relatively new diagnosis that was added to the DSM-5 in 2013. It is often comorbid with other mental health disorders such as ADHD, anxiety, and depression. Children with DMDD may experience intense emotional dysregulation, leading to frequent outbursts that can be physically and emotionally exhausting for both the child and their parents. It is important for parents to understand that these behaviors are not the result of poor parenting or a lack of discipline, but rather a symptom of a complex neurological disorder.

Once parents have a clear understanding of DMDD, they can begin to set realistic expectations and goals for their child. This starts with acknowledging the child's strengths and limitations. Children with DMDD often have difficulty with impulse control, emotional regulation, and social interactions. However, they may also possess unique strengths such as creativity, empathy, and intelligence. By recognizing and nurturing these strengths, parents can help their child build a sense of self-worth and confidence, which can in turn help them manage their symptoms.

When setting goals for a child with DMDD, it is important to start small and focus on achievable objectives. This might include things like improving communication skills, developing coping strategies, or building a stronger relationship with family members. Parents should work collaboratively with their child's mental health professionals to identify specific goals that are appropriate for their child's age and developmental level. It is also important to be flexible and willing to adjust goals as needed. Progress may be slow and incremental, but even small successes can be cause for celebration and encouragement.

Another key aspect of setting realistic expectations and goals is to avoid comparison to other children. It can be tempting for parents to compare their child's behavior to that of their peers or siblings, but this can be demoralizing and counterproductive. Children with DMDD are dealing with a unique set of challenges that require a specialized approach. It is important for parents to focus on their own child's progress and growth, rather than comparing them to others.

In order to effectively manage DMDD, parents must also set realistic expectations for themselves. This includes recognizing their own limitations and seeking support when needed. Parenting a child with DMDD can be incredibly challenging, and it is important for parents to prioritize self-care and seek out resources and support from mental health professionals, support groups, and other parents who are going through similar experiences.

Overall, setting realistic expectations and goals is an essential component of effective parenting for children with DMDD. By understanding the nature of the disorder, acknowledging the child's strengths and limitations, and working collaboratively with mental health professionals, parents can help their child build important life skills, develop positive relationships, and achieve their full potential. While progress may be slow and incremental, even small successes can be cause for celebration and encouragement, and can help parents and children alike feel more confident and empowered.

Encouraging Positive Behaviors

Encouraging positive behaviors is an essential aspect of effective parenting, particularly when navigating DMDD at home. DMDD, or Disruptive Mood Dysregulation

Disorder, is a neurodevelopmental disorder that affects children's ability to regulate their emotions and behavior. Children with DMDD may display intense and frequent temper tantrums, irritability, and other disruptive behaviors. These behaviors can be challenging for parents and caregivers to manage, but there are strategies that can help encourage positive behaviors in children with DMDD.

One of the most effective ways to encourage positive behaviors is through positive reinforcement. Positive reinforcement involves rewarding a child for displaying desirable behaviors, such as following rules, managing their emotions, and communicating effectively. Rewards can take many forms, such as praise, privileges, or tokens that can be exchanged for prizes. When children are consistently rewarded for positive behaviors, they are more likely to continue exhibiting those behaviors.

It is important to note that positive reinforcement should be specific and immediate. For example, if a child with DMDD has a history of aggressive behavior, parents might reward them with praise and a small token, such as a sticker, for managing their emotions during a frustrating situation. The reward should be given immediately after the positive behavior is displayed to ensure that the child understands the connection between the behavior and the reward.

Another effective way to encourage positive behaviors is through modeling. Parents can model positive behaviors by managing their own emotions and responding calmly to frustrating situations. This can help children with DMDD learn how to regulate their own emotions and behaviors. Additionally, parents can model positive behaviors by communicating effectively and setting clear boundaries. When children see their parents communicating respectfully and setting boundaries, they are more likely to do the same.

Setting clear expectations is another important way to encourage positive behaviors in children with DMDD. Parents should communicate their expectations clearly and consistently, and provide specific examples of what those expectations look like in practice. For example, if a parent expects their child to manage their emotions when frustrated, they might provide specific strategies for doing so, such as taking deep breaths or counting to 10. When children have clear expectations and know what is expected of them, they are more likely to exhibit positive behaviors.

Consistency is key when encouraging positive behaviors in children with DMDD. Parents should be consistent in their expectations, their rewards, and their consequences. When children know that positive behaviors will be rewarded and negative behaviors will be met with consequences, they are more likely to exhibit positive behaviors.

It is also important to remember that children with DMDD may need additional support to manage their emotions and behaviors. Parents should work closely with mental health professionals to develop a comprehensive treatment plan that addresses the child's individual needs. This may include therapy, medication, or other interventions.

In addition to these strategies, parents can also encourage positive behaviors by creating a positive and supportive home environment. This includes creating a routine and structure, providing opportunities for positive social interactions, and fostering a sense of belonging and security. Children are more likely to demonstrate good behaviors when they feel safe and supported..

Encouraging positive behaviors in children with DMDD can be challenging, but with patience, consistency, and support, it is possible. By using strategies such as positive reinforcement, modeling, setting clear expectations, and creating a supportive home environment, parents can help their children develop the skills they need to regulate their emotions and behaviors. It is important to remember that progress may be slow and incremental, but even small successes can be cause for celebration and encouragement. With time, effort, and support, children with DMDD can learn to manage their emotions and behaviors and thrive in their home and community.

Promoting Self-esteem and Resilience

Promoting self-esteem and resilience is an important part of effective parenting, particularly when navigating DMDD at home. DMDD, or Disruptive Mood Dysregulation Disorder, is a neurodevelopmental disorder that affects children's ability to regulate their emotions and behavior. Children with DMDD may struggle with self-esteem and resilience due to the challenges they face in managing their emotions and behaviors. However, there are strategies parents can use to promote self-esteem and resilience in their children.

One of the most effective ways to promote self-esteem and resilience is to provide children with opportunities for success. When children with DMDD experience success, it can help build their self-confidence and self-esteem. Parents can provide opportunities for success by setting achievable goals, providing support and encouragement, and celebrating their child's accomplishments. For example, if a child with DMDD struggles with managing their emotions, parents might set a goal for them to take deep breaths when they feel frustrated. When the child is successful in meeting this goal, parents can provide praise and positive reinforcement to build their self-esteem.

Another important way to promote self-esteem and resilience is to foster a positive self-image. Parents can help their children develop a positive self-image by encouraging them to focus on their strengths and abilities, rather than their weaknesses or limitations. For example, if a child with DMDD struggles with social interactions, parents can help them identify their strengths in other areas, such as academics or sports. When children feel good about themselves and their abilities, they are more likely to exhibit resilience in the face of challenges.

Parents can also promote self-esteem and resilience by providing emotional support and validation. Children with DMDD may struggle with emotional regulation and may feel misunderstood or invalidated by others. Parents can provide emotional support by actively listening to their child, acknowledging their feelings, and offering support and encouragement. For example, if a child with DMDD is upset about a frustrating situation, parents can offer validation by saying "I understand why you feel upset. It's okay to feel that way, and I am here to support you." When children feel emotionally supported, they are more likely to exhibit resilience in the face of difficult situations.

In addition to these strategies, parents can also promote self-esteem and resilience by teaching their children coping skills. Coping skills are tools and strategies that children can use to manage their emotions and behaviors. Parents can teach coping skills by modeling healthy coping strategies, such as taking deep breaths or going for a walk to manage stress. Additionally, parents can work with mental health professionals to develop a comprehensive treatment plan that includes coping skills training.

Finally, it is important to remember that promoting self-esteem and resilience is a long-term process. Children with DMDD may face significant challenges in managing their emotions and behaviors, and it may take time for them to develop self-esteem and resilience. Parents should be patient, consistent, and supportive, and celebrate small successes along the way. Even small accomplishments can help build a child's self-esteem and resilience.

Using Positive Reinforcement Effectively

Effective parenting requires a multifaceted approach, and one of the most powerful tools in a parent's toolkit is positive reinforcement. Positive reinforcement is the process of rewarding positive behaviors with praise, affection, or other types of rewards, in order to encourage the child to repeat that behavior in the future. When used effectively, positive reinforcement can help parents navigate the challenges of DMDD at home, helping to promote positive behaviors and manage disruptive or challenging behaviors.

Positive reinforcement is particularly effective when it is specific, immediate, and consistent. For example, if a child with DMDD is struggling to manage their anger and frustration, a parent might use positive reinforcement by praising the child when they are able to calm down and use a coping skill. The praise should be specific, such as "I am proud of you for taking deep breaths and calming down. That shows real maturity." The praise should be immediate, so that the child associates the positive behavior with the reward. And the praise should be consistent, so that the child knows what to expect and is motivated to continue exhibiting positive behaviors.

Another effective way to use positive reinforcement is to pair it with a token economy system. A token economy system is a way of providing tangible rewards, such as stickers or points, for positive behaviors. Parents can use a token economy system to motivate children with DMDD to exhibit positive behaviors, such as following rules or using coping skills. For example, a parent might create a chart with a list of positive behaviors, and each time the child exhibits one of those behaviors, they earn a sticker or point. After earning a certain number of stickers or points, the child can trade them in for a larger reward, such as extra screen time or a favorite activity.

It is important to note that positive reinforcement should be used in conjunction with other parenting strategies, such as setting clear expectations and consequences for negative behaviors. Positive reinforcement should not be used as a way to bribe or manipulate children, but rather as a way to encourage positive behaviors and build a positive relationship between parent and child.

One important consideration when using positive reinforcement is the type of rewards that are used. While tangible rewards can be effective, it is important to also use non-tangible rewards such as praise and affection. Over-reliance on tangible rewards can actually undermine the effectiveness of positive reinforcement over time, and children may become less motivated to exhibit positive behaviors without the promise of a tangible reward.

It is also important to use positive reinforcement in a way that is developmentally appropriate for the child. Younger children may be motivated by simple rewards such as stickers or treats, while older children may prefer rewards such as extra privileges or activities. It is important to adjust the rewards to match the child's interests and developmental level.

Finally, it is important to use positive reinforcement in a way that is culturally sensitive and respectful. Different cultures may have different ideas about what is appropriate to reward or praise, and it is important for parents to be aware of these differences and adjust their approach accordingly.

Part IV

Behavioral and Therapeutic Interventions

When it comes to managing DMDD in children, behavioral and therapeutic interventions can be valuable tools for parents. These interventions are designed to help children develop coping skills, manage their emotions, and improve their behavior. Effective parenting strategies for navigating DMDD at home can include implementing these interventions in a way that is tailored to the child's needs and preferences. This can involve working with a therapist or counselor, creating a behavior plan with clear expectations and consequences, and using positive reinforcement to encourage positive behaviors. By incorporating behavioral and therapeutic interventions into their parenting approach, parents can help their children with DMDD thrive and succeed.

Medications for DMDD

Disruptive Mood Dysregulation Disorder (DMDD) is a condition that can be challenging to manage, and in some cases, medications may be prescribed to help alleviate some of the symptoms. Effective parenting strategies for navigating DMDD at home should include an understanding of the medications that may be prescribed and how they work.

There are a few different types of medications that may be prescribed for children with DMDD, including antidepressants, mood stabilizers, and atypical antipsychotics. Antidepressants can help regulate mood and alleviate symptoms of anxiety and depression, while mood stabilizers can help control mood swings and reduce impulsivity. Atypical antipsychotics may be used in cases where symptoms are severe and disruptive, and they can help regulate emotions and reduce aggression.

While medications can be helpful in managing symptoms of DMDD, it's important to understand that they are not a cure, and they can come with potential side effects. Parents should work closely with their child's healthcare provider to understand the potential risks and benefits of any medication that is prescribed and to monitor their child's response to the medication.

It's also important to remember that medication is just one part of a comprehensive treatment plan for DMDD. Effective parenting strategies for navigating DMDD at home should include a combination of medication, therapy, and behavioral interventions to help children manage their symptoms and develop coping skills.

Parents can play an important role in helping their child with DMDD take medication as prescribed and monitor for any side effects. This may involve setting reminders for medication times, keeping track of any changes in behavior or mood, and communicating regularly with their child's healthcare provider.

In addition to working closely with healthcare providers, parents can also support their child with DMDD by creating a calm and structured home environment. This can include establishing consistent routines, setting clear expectations and boundaries, and providing opportunities for their child to engage in positive activities that promote well-being.

Finally, it's important for parents to take care of their own mental health and well-being when navigating DMDD with their child. This may involve seeking support from a therapist or counselor, joining a support group for parents of children with DMDD, or practicing self-care activities like exercise, meditation, or hobbies.

Cognitive-Behavioral Therapy and Other Therapeutic Approaches

Cognitive-behavioral therapy (CBT) is a type of therapy that is often used to treat mental health conditions in children and adults, including disruptive mood dysregulation disorder (DMDD). CBT is a structured, short-term therapy that is designed to help individuals change negative thought patterns and behaviors that are causing distress and interfering with daily life. CBT can be a valuable tool in managing DMDD symptoms and helping children develop healthy coping strategies.

CBT typically involves several stages, including assessment, goal setting, and skill building. During the assessment phase, the therapist will work with the child to identify negative thought patterns and behaviors that are contributing to their DMDD symptoms. The therapist will also help the child set specific, achievable goals for the therapy.

During the skill-building phase, the therapist will teach the child specific skills and strategies to manage their DMDD symptoms. These may include relaxation techniques, cognitive restructuring, and problem-solving skills. The therapist may also work with the child to develop a behavior plan that includes clear expectations and consequences for positive and negative behaviors.

In addition to CBT, there are other therapeutic approaches that can be helpful in managing DMDD symptoms. Dialectical behavior therapy (DBT) is a type of therapy that is often used to treat borderline personality disorder, but can also be effective in treating DMDD. DBT focuses on the development of mindfulness, emotion control, distress tolerance, and interpersonal effectiveness skills.

Parent-child interaction therapy (PCIT) is another therapeutic approach that can be effective in managing DMDD. PCIT is a structured, short-term therapy that focuses on improving parent-child interactions and communication. The therapist works with the parent and child together to teach positive parenting strategies, such as active listening and positive reinforcement.

Play therapy is another therapeutic approach that can be helpful in managing DMDD symptoms in younger children. Play therapy involves using toys and other materials to help the child express their emotions and work through their challenges in a non-threatening, non-judgmental environment.

Effective parenting strategies for navigating DMDD at home when using therapeutic approaches can involve working closely with the therapist or counselor to reinforce the skills and strategies learned in therapy. Parents can also implement positive parenting strategies, such as clear expectations, consistent consequences, and positive reinforcement, to support their child's progress.

Parents can also encourage healthy coping strategies, such as deep breathing and mindfulness exercises, to help their child manage their emotions and prevent escalation of negative feelings. It is important for parents to be patient and supportive as their child works through therapy and to communicate regularly with their child's healthcare team to ensure that they are receiving the best possible care.

In summary, cognitive-behavioral therapy and other therapeutic approaches can be valuable tools in managing DMDD symptoms in children. These approaches focus on helping children develop healthy coping strategies and manage their emotions in a positive way. Effective parenting strategies for navigating DMDD at home can involve working closely with the therapist, implementing positive parenting strategies, and encouraging healthy coping strategies. With a comprehensive approach to managing DMDD, children can thrive and succeed.

How to Find and Work with Mental Health Professionals

Finding and working with mental health professionals can be a daunting task, but it is essential for parents of children with disruptive mood dysregulation disorder (DMDD) to have a supportive team in place to help manage their child's condition. Here are some tips on how to find and work with mental health professionals:

Ask for referrals: Start by asking for referrals from your child's pediatrician, school counselor, or other healthcare providers. They may have a network of trusted mental health professionals to recommend.

Check your insurance coverage: Before scheduling an appointment, check with your insurance provider to see what mental health services are covered under your plan. This will help you narrow down your search to providers who accept your insurance.

Research potential providers: Once you have a list of potential providers, do some research to learn more about their credentials and experience. Look up their licensure status and any disciplinary actions on your state's licensing board website. You can also search for reviews and ratings on online directories or ask for recommendations from friends and family members.

Schedule a consultation: Before committing to a provider, schedule a consultation to meet with them and discuss your child's needs and goals. This can also give you an opportunity to gauge their approach and communication style to see if it is a good fit for your family.

Ask questions: During the consultation or initial appointment, don't be afraid to ask questions to better understand the provider's approach and expertise. Ask about their experience working with children with DMDD specifically, their treatment philosophy, and their availability for appointments.

Work collaboratively: Effective treatment for DMDD often involves a collaborative effort between the mental health professional, parents, and other healthcare providers involved in the child's care. Be open and honest about your child's symptoms, behaviors, and needs, and work with the provider to develop a comprehensive treatment plan.

Stay engaged: It's important to stay engaged and involved in your child's treatment, even if they are seeing a mental health professional independently. Attend appointments, communicate regularly with the provider, and follow through on recommended strategies and techniques at home.

When working with a mental health professional to manage DMDD, effective parenting strategies can also play a critical role in supporting the child's overall wellbeing. Parents can work with the provider to reinforce the skills and techniques learned in therapy, and communicate regularly with the provider to ensure that they are staying on track with treatment goals. They can also create a structured environment that emphasizes positive reinforcement and clear expectations, and encourage healthy coping strategies such as mindfulness exercises and physical activity.

In summary, finding and working with mental health professionals can be an important step in managing DMDD in children. By doing research, asking questions, and staying engaged in the treatment process, parents can work collaboratively with their child's provider to develop an effective treatment plan. By implementing effective parenting strategies at home, parents can reinforce the skills learned in therapy and support their child's overall wellbeing.

Part V

Managing Challenging Behaviors

Managing challenging behaviors can be a daunting task for parents, especially when dealing with children who have disruptive mood dysregulation disorder (DMDD). DMDD is a condition that causes children to have frequent and severe temper outbursts, leading to problems in daily functioning. Effective parenting strategies can help parents navigate these behaviors at home and create a more harmonious household. By understanding the triggers of DMDD and implementing positive reinforcement techniques, parents can provide a stable and supportive environment for their children. In this context, managing challenging behaviors is not about punishing or controlling the child, but about guiding and empowering them to express their emotions in a healthy way.

Strategies for Dealing with Anger and Aggression

Anger and aggression are common challenges faced by parents of children with disruptive mood dysregulation disorder (DMDD). These behaviors can be disruptive to the family and cause distress to the child, who may struggle to regulate their emotions. Effective parenting strategies can help parents navigate these behaviors and support their child in developing healthy coping mechanisms. In this article, we will explore strategies for dealing with anger and aggression in children with DMDD.

Understanding the Triggers

The first step in managing challenging behaviors is to understand the triggers that lead to them. Children with DMDD are more sensitive to stress and can become overwhelmed easily. As a result, seemingly minor events can trigger intense emotional reactions. Parents can work with their child to identify the situations that tend to trigger anger and aggression. Once these triggers are identified, parents can help their child develop coping mechanisms to manage their emotions.

Positive Reinforcement

Positive reinforcement is an effective and powerful tool in shaping behavior. Children with DMDD respond well to praise and rewards for positive behavior. Parents can use positive reinforcement to encourage their child to engage in appropriate behavior. For example, parents can offer praise and rewards when their child handles a difficult situation without becoming angry or aggressive. Over time, positive reinforcement can help children learn to regulate their emotions and behavior.

Modeling Calmness

Children learn by example, and parents can model calmness and self-control to help their child manage their emotions. When parents become angry or frustrated, it can be difficult for the child to remain calm. By modeling calmness and self-control, parents can show their child how to manage their emotions effectively. This can be challenging, especially when parents are dealing with challenging behaviors. However, by remaining calm and modeling positive behavior, parents can help their child learn to manage their emotions in a healthy way.

De-Escalation Techniques

When a child becomes angry or aggressive, it is important to de-escalate the situation to prevent it from escalating further. De-escalation techniques involve using calming techniques to help the child regain control of their emotions. These techniques can include deep breathing exercises, counting to 10, or using calming words or phrases. Parents can work with their child to identify the techniques that work best for them. By practicing these techniques, the child can learn to calm themselves down when they feel overwhelmed.

Effective Communication

Effective communication is essential when dealing with challenging behaviors. Parents should communicate in a calm and respectful manner, using positive language to encourage their child. Instead of criticizing their child's behavior, parents can use positive language to reinforce positive behavior. For example, instead of saying "stop being so angry," parents can say "I appreciate how you're trying to control your anger." By using positive language, parents can encourage their child to continue using positive coping mechanisms.

Consistency

Consistency is key when dealing with challenging behaviors. Children with DMDD respond well to routine and structure. Parents should establish clear rules and consequences for their child's behavior. It is important to be consistent in enforcing these rules and consequences. By providing a structured environment, children with DMDD can learn to manage their emotions and behavior more effectively.

Seeking Professional Help

Parents of children with DMDD may benefit from seeking professional help. A mental health professional can work with the child to develop coping mechanisms and strategies for managing their emotions. They can also provide support and guidance for parents, helping them to better understand their child's behavior and develop effective parenting strategies. If parents are struggling to manage their child's behavior, they should not hesitate to seek professional help.

Tips for Managing Emotional Outbursts

Emotional outbursts are a common occurrence in children with disruptive mood dysregulation disorder (DMDD). These outbursts can be challenging for parents to manage, but with the right strategies, it is possible to help children regulate their emotions and minimize the impact of these outbursts on family life.

One of the most important strategies for managing emotional outbursts is to remain calm and patient. Children with DMDD may struggle to regulate their emotions, which can lead to frequent and intense outbursts. It is important for parents to stay calm and avoid reacting emotionally to their child's behavior. Instead, parents should strive to remain patient and provide a supportive and empathetic environment.

Another effective strategy for managing emotional outbursts is to validate the child's emotions. Children with DMDD may feel overwhelmed by their emotions, and it is important for parents to acknowledge and validate these feelings. This can be done by using active listening skills, such as repeating back what the child has said or acknowledging the child's feelings.

In addition to validation, it is important to help the child identify and label their emotions. This can be done by asking questions about how the child is feeling, and helping them to identify the specific emotions they are experiencing. This can help the child develop a greater understanding of their emotions and develop coping strategies to manage them.

Another effective strategy for managing emotional outbursts is to provide a safe space for the child to express their emotions. This may involve creating a quiet space where the child can go to calm down or providing tools such as fidget toys or stress balls to help them release tension. It is also important to encourage the child to express their emotions through words rather than physical outbursts.

Positive reinforcement is another effective strategy for managing emotional outbursts. This involves rewarding positive behaviors, such as using words to express emotions or seeking help when feeling overwhelmed. Positive reinforcement helps to encourage the child to continue exhibiting these behaviors, ultimately leading to a decrease in negative behaviors.

Establishing a consistent routine and structure is also important for managing emotional outbursts. Children with DMDD may struggle with transitions or changes in routine, which can lead to increased anxiety and irritability. A consistent routine can help to provide a sense of stability and predictability, reducing the likelihood of emotional outbursts.

In some cases, it may be necessary to implement consequences for negative behaviors. However, it is important to ensure that consequences are appropriate and not overly punitive. Consequences should be clearly communicated and should focus on helping the child learn from their actions rather than simply punishing them.

Finally, it is important for parents to seek support when managing emotional outbursts in their child. This may involve seeking the help of a therapist or counselor who can provide guidance and support in managing difficult behaviors. Support groups can also be a valuable resource, allowing parents to connect with others who are facing similar challenges and share strategies and tips for managing emotional outbursts.

How to Handle difficult situations in Public

andling difficult situations in public can be a challenge for any parent, but it can be especially challenging for parents of children with disruptive mood dysregulation disorder (DMDD). Children with DMDD may struggle to regulate their emotions, leading to frequent and intense outbursts in public settings. However, with the right strategies and preparation, parents can effectively handle difficult situations in public and help their child manage their emotions.

One of the most important strategies for handling difficult situations in public is to plan ahead. This involves anticipating potential triggers for your child's emotional outbursts and having a plan in place for how to manage these situations. For example, if your child becomes over stimulated in loud or crowded environments, you may want to avoid these settings or plan for a quiet space where your child can go to calm down.

It is also important to establish clear boundaries and expectations with your child. This may involve setting rules for appropriate behavior in public settings, such as using inside voices and keeping hands to oneself. Clear expectations and boundaries can help to prevent difficult situations from occurring and provide a framework for managing these situations when they do occur.

Another effective strategy for handling difficult situations in public is to remain calm and composed. Children with DMDD may struggle to regulate their emotions, but it is important for parents to model calm and composed behavior. This can help to de-escalate the situation and provide a sense of stability and safety for the child.

It is also important to be prepared with coping strategies for managing emotional outbursts in public. This may involve having calming tools on hand, such as stress balls or fidget toys, or practicing deep breathing techniques with your child. Coping strategies can help your child manage their emotions and prevent outbursts from escalating.

In some cases, it may be necessary to remove your child from the situation to prevent a full-blown emotional outburst. This may involve taking your child to a quiet area or leaving the public setting altogether. It is important to have a plan in place for how to handle these situations and communicate this plan to your child ahead of time.

Positive reinforcement can also be an effective strategy for handling difficult situations in public. This involves rewarding positive behaviors and acknowledging when your child is making an effort to regulate their emotions.

For example, you may praise your child for using their coping strategies or calmly communicating their feelings.

It is also important to remember that other people may not understand your child's condition or behavior. This can be frustrating and isolating for parents, but it is important to remain calm and advocate for your child's needs. This may involve educating others about DMDD and the challenges that your child faces or simply asking for understanding and patience.

Finally, it is important to seek support when handling difficult situations in public. This may involve seeking the help of a therapist or counselor who can provide guidance and support in managing difficult behaviors. Support groups can also be a valuable resource, allowing parents to connect with others who are facing similar challenges and share strategies and tips for handling difficult situations in public.

Ways to Handle Setbacks and Relapses

Setbacks and relapses are a common occurrence when navigating disruptive mood dysregulation disorder (DMDD) at home. Despite the best efforts of parents and healthcare professionals, children with DMDD may experience setbacks and relapses in their treatment. However, with the right strategies, it is possible to handle setbacks and relapses in a positive and effective manner.

One of the most important strategies for handling setbacks and relapses is to remain optimistic and focused on the long-term goal of managing the child's DMDD symptoms. It can be easy to become discouraged or feel like progress is not being made when a setback or relapse occurs, but it is important to remember that recovery is a journey, not a destination. By remaining focused on the long-term goal, parents can help their child stay motivated and maintain a positive outlook.

Another effective strategy is to identify the triggers or factors that may have contributed to the setback or relapse. This may involve working with a healthcare professional to analyze the child's treatment plan and identify areas where adjustments may be needed. By addressing the underlying causes of the setback or relapse, parents can help their child avoid similar situations in the future.

It is also important to have a support system in place when handling setbacks and relapses. This may involve connecting with other parents who have children with DMDD, or seeking the help of a therapist or counselor who can provide guidance and support. Support groups and therapy sessions can be valuable resources for parents who are struggling to manage setbacks and relapses in their child's treatment.

Another effective strategy is to practice self-care. Parenting a child with DMDD can be emotionally and physically exhausting, and it is important for parents to take care of their own needs in order to provide the best possible care for their child. This may involve taking time for exercise, relaxation, or pursuing hobbies and interests. By taking care of their own needs, parents can help reduce stress and increase their ability to handle setbacks and relapses in their child's treatment.

It is also important for parents to stay flexible and adaptable in their approach to managing DMDD. What may work one day may not work the next, and it is important to be willing to try new approaches and make adjustments to the treatment plan as needed. By staying open to new ideas and approaches, parents can help their child continue to make progress in managing their DMDD symptoms.

Another effective strategy is to use positive reinforcement and celebrate successes, no matter how small they may seem. Celebrating successes can help to maintain a positive outlook and provide motivation for continuing to work towards managing DMDD symptoms. This can involve using a reward system for positive behaviors or celebrating milestones in treatment.

Finally, it is important for parents to communicate openly and honestly with their child about setbacks and relapses.

This can help to reduce feelings of shame or embarrassment and foster a sense of teamwork in managing DMDD. By communicating openly and honestly, parents can help their child feel supported and encouraged in their journey towards managing their DMDD symptoms.

In conclusion, setbacks and relapses are a common occurrence when managing disruptive mood dysregulation disorder (DMDD) at home. However, by remaining optimistic, identifying triggers, having a support system in place, practicing self-care, staying flexible and adaptable, using positive reinforcement, celebrating successes, and communicating openly and honestly, parents can effectively handle setbacks and relapses and help their child continue to make progress in managing their DMDD symptoms. Effective parenting strategies are essential for navigating DMDD at home, and by working together with their child and healthcare professionals, parents can provide the support and guidance needed to help their child thrive.

Part VI

Moving Forward

Moving forward is essential when it comes to effective parenting strategies for navigating DMDD at home. It's important to remember that those with DMDD can learn to manage their emotions and behaviors. Parents need to provide unconditional love and support, along with consistent, structured routines. Teaching anger management and problem-solving skills can help children learn to cope with their emotions. Parents should also be willing to adjust discipline styles to fit the needs of their child. It is important to remember to stay calm and stay consistent when dealing with challenging behaviors. With patience, dedication, and a willingness to continue trying, parents can successfully navigate DMDD and help their children move forward.

Celebrating successes and progress

Celebrating successes and progress is an essential aspect of effective parenting strategies for navigating DMDD at home. Children with DMDD often struggle with emotional regulation, leading to frequent outbursts and behavioral challenges. However, by recognizing and celebrating their successes and progress, parents can reinforce positive behavior and build their child's self-esteem.

Here are some tips for celebrating successes and progress with your child:

Set achievable goals: Set realistic goals with your child that are achievable and measurable. This can include academic goals, behavioral goals, or personal goals. By setting achievable goals, you can help your child build confidence and a sense of accomplishment.

Recognize small successes: Celebrate small successes and progress regularly, even if they are minor. This can include completing homework without assistance, demonstrating self-control during a challenging situation, or showing empathy towards others. By recognizing and celebrating small successes, you can reinforce positive behavior and build your child's self-esteem.

Use positive reinforcement: Positive reinforcement is a great tool for encouraging positive behavior. This can include verbal praise, physical affection, or small rewards such as stickers or extra screen time. By using positive reinforcement, you can reinforce positive behavior and encourage your child to continue making progress.

Involve the whole family: Celebrating successes and progress can be a family affair. Involve siblings and other family members in recognizing and celebrating your child's successes. This can create a supportive and positive environment that encourages positive behavior.

Focus on effort, not just outcome: When celebrating successes and progress, it's important to focus on the effort and hard work that went into achieving the goal, not just the outcome. This can help your child build resilience and a growth mindset, which can be particularly important for children with DMDD who may struggle with emotional regulation.

Be specific: When recognizing and celebrating your child's successes and progress, be specific about what they did well. This can help them understand exactly what behavior you are reinforcing and encourage them to continue making progress in that area.

Reflect on progress: Take time to reflect on your child's progress over time. This can include reviewing behavioral charts or academic progress reports. By reflecting on progress, you can recognize how far your child has come and encourage them to continue making progress.

By celebrating successes and progress with your child, you can reinforce positive behavior, build their self-esteem, and create a supportive and positive environment at home. Celebrating successes and progress can be particularly important for children with DMDD, who may struggle with emotional regulation and have a negative self-image. By focusing on effort, being specific, and involving the whole family, parents can create a culture of positivity and support that encourages positive behavior and helps their child thrive.

Preparing for the Future

Preparing for the future can be a daunting task, especially for parents who have children with Disruptive Mood Dysregulation Disorder (DMDD). DMDD is a relatively new diagnosis that was introduced in the DSM-5 in 2013. It is a disorder that affects children and adolescents, and it is often characterized by severe and recurrent temper outbursts or tantrums that are grossly out of proportion to the situation. DMDD can have a significant impact on a child's life, and effective parenting strategies are necessary to navigate this disorder at home.

As a parent, preparing for the future means setting your child up for success despite their diagnosis. This requires a multifaceted approach that involves understanding your child's diagnosis, accessing appropriate treatment, and implementing effective parenting strategies. It is essential to recognize that every child is unique and that their treatment and parenting strategies need to be tailored to their specific needs.

The first step in preparing for the future is understanding your child's diagnosis. DMDD is a relatively new diagnosis, and many parents may not be familiar with it. It is important to research the disorder and learn about the symptoms, treatment options, and possible outcomes. Understanding your child's diagnosis can help you make informed decisions about their treatment and parenting strategies.

The second step is accessing appropriate treatment. DMDD is a complex disorder that requires a comprehensive treatment approach. Treatment options may include therapy, medication and lifestyle changes. It is essential to work closely with your child's healthcare provider to develop a treatment plan that meets their unique needs. This may involve trying different medications, attending therapy sessions, and making lifestyle changes such as regular exercise and a healthy diet.

The third step is implementing effective parenting strategies. DMDD can be challenging to navigate at home, and it is essential to develop strategies that promote positive behavior and reduce the frequency and severity of temper outbursts. Also, preparing for the future might also mean recognizing that your child's needs may change over time. It is essential to stay informed about new research and treatment options and to work closely with your child's healthcare provider to adjust their treatment plan as needed.

Finally, preparing for the future means planning for their child's long-term success. Children with DMDD often struggle with social interactions, and parents can help them develop social skills by encouraging them to participate in group activities or sports. They can also help their child develop their interests and talents by providing opportunities for them to explore their passions.

Finding ongoing support and resources

Parenting can be a challenging and rewarding experience, but when a child is diagnosed with Disruptive Mood Dysregulation Disorder (DMDD), it can add extra stress and frustration to the process. DMDD is a disorder that affects children and adolescents, causing severe temper outbursts that are out of proportion to the situation at hand. Parents may find it difficult to navigate their child's behavior and may feel overwhelmed and isolated. However, with the right support and resources, parents can effectively manage their child's DMDD and help their child thrive.

One important aspect of finding ongoing support is to connect with a mental health professional who has experience working with children with DMDD. A therapist or counselor can provide guidance on effective parenting strategies, such as using positive reinforcement, setting clear boundaries, and teaching coping skills. They can also provide a safe and supportive space for parents to discuss their concerns and frustrations.

In addition to therapy, support groups can be a valuable resource for parents of children with DMDD. These groups allow parents to connect with others who are going through similar experiences, share tips and advice, and offer emotional support. Online support groups, such as those found on social media or through mental health organizations, can be particularly helpful for parents who may not have access to in-person groups in their area.

Another important resource for parents is education. Learning about DMDD and its symptoms can help parents better understand their child's behavior and develop effective strategies for managing it. There are many books and online resources available that provide information on DMDD, as well as parenting tips and strategies. Parents may also benefit from attending workshops or classes on parenting children with DMDD, which can be offered through mental health organizations or community centers.

In addition to seeking out professional support, parents can also take steps to create a supportive home environment for their child. This may involve setting clear routines and schedules, creating a calm and structured environment, and using positive reinforcement to encourage positive behavior. It's important for parents to communicate openly and honestly with their child, expressing their love and support while also setting clear expectations for behavior.

Finally, parents should prioritize their own self-care. Caring for a child with DMDD can be emotionally and physically draining, and parents need to take care of themselves in order to be effective caregivers. This may involve taking time for self-care activities, such as exercise or meditation, seeking out their own therapy or support groups, and reaching out to friends and family for support.

CONCLUSION

As we come to the end of this book on Effective Parenting Strategies for Navigating DMDD at Home, it is important to reflect on the journey we have taken together. We started by exploring what DMDD is and how it affects children and families. We then dove into effective parenting strategies, such as setting clear boundaries, using positive reinforcement, and teaching coping skills. Throughout this book, we emphasized the importance of seeking professional support, connecting with support groups, educating oneself on DMDD, creating a supportive home environment, and prioritizing self-care.

Parenting a child with DMDD can be a challenging and often overwhelming experience. The unpredictable and intense mood swings, temper outbursts, and emotional dysregulation can leave parents feeling helpless and frustrated. However, as we have seen throughout this book, there are many effective parenting strategies that can help parents navigate their child's DMDD and create a supportive and loving home environment.

One of the key takeaways from this book is the importance of seeking professional support. A mental health professional who has experience working with children with DMDD can provide guidance and support to both the child and the parent. They can help parents develop effective parenting strategies, such as using positive reinforcement, setting clear boundaries, and teaching coping skills. They can also provide a safe and supportive space for parents to discuss their concerns and frustrations.

Another important resource for parents is support groups. These groups allow parents to connect with others who are going through similar experiences, share tips and advice, and offer emotional support. Online support groups, such as those found on social media or through mental health organizations, can be particularly helpful for parents who may not have access to in-person groups in their area.

Education is also a key component of effective parenting strategies for navigating DMDD at home. Learning about DMDD and its symptoms can help parents better understand their child's behavior and develop effective strategies for managing it. There are many books and online resources available that provide information on DMDD, as well as parenting tips and strategies. Parents may also benefit from attending workshops or classes on parenting children with DMDD, which can be offered through mental health organizations or community centers.

Creating a supportive home environment is another important aspect of effective parenting strategies for navigating DMDD at home. This may involve setting clear routines and schedules, creating a calm and structured environment, and using positive reinforcement to encourage positive behavior. It's important for parents to communicate openly and honestly with their child, expressing their love and support while also setting clear expectations for behavior.

Finally, parents should prioritize their own self-care. Caring for a child with DMDD can be emotionally and physically draining, and parents need to take care of themselves in order to be effective caregivers. This may involve taking time for self-care activities, such as exercise or meditation, seeking out their own therapy or support groups, and reaching out to friends and family for support.

Throughout this book, we have emphasized the importance of understanding, supporting, and empowering children with DMDD. It is important for parents to recognize that their child's behavior is not a reflection of their parenting or their child's character. DMDD is a medical condition that requires treatment and support. By understanding and accepting their child's condition, parents can support their child in managing their emotions and behavior.

Empowering children with DMDD means helping them develop coping skills and strategies for managing their emotions. This may involve teaching them deep breathing exercises, mindfulness techniques, or other relaxation techniques. It may also involve working with a mental health professional to develop a personalized treatment plan that addresses the child's specific needs.

As we conclude this book, we hope that it has provided valuable insights and strategies for parents of children with DMDD. It is our belief that with the right support and resources, parents can effectively manage their child's DMDD.

Mood Tracker

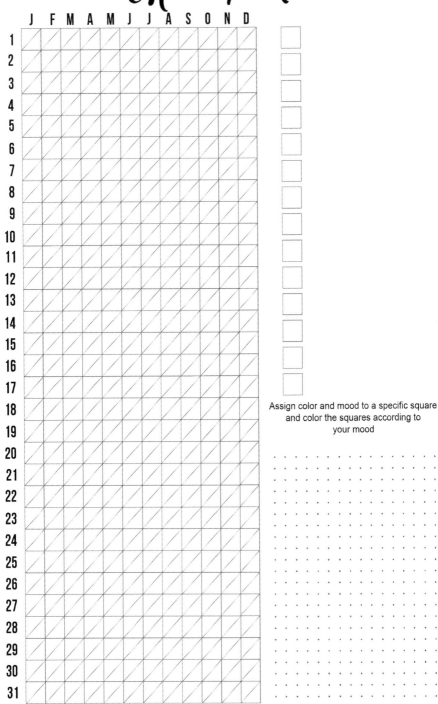

Assign color and mood to a specific square
and color the squares according to
your mood

Mood Tracker

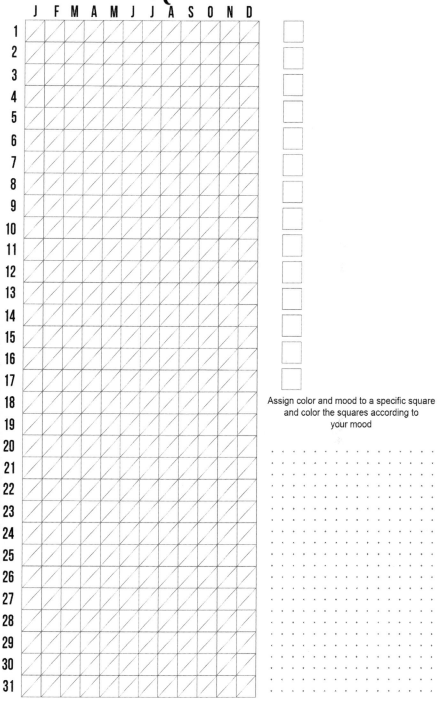

Assign color and mood to a specific square
and color the squares according to
your mood

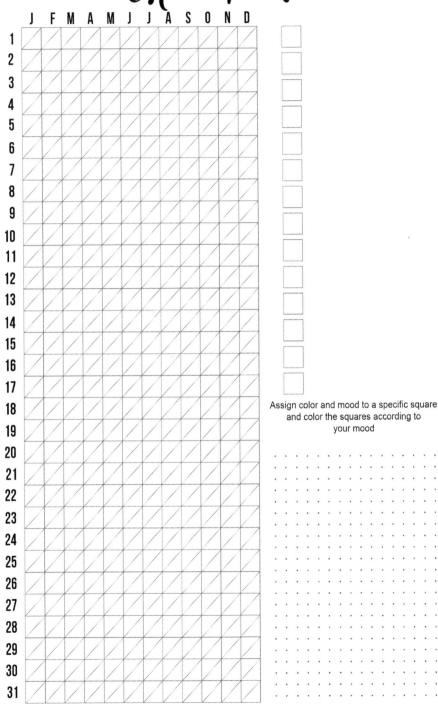

Mood Tracker

	J	F	M	A	M	J	J	A	S	O	N	D
1												
2												
3												
4												
5												
6												
7												
8												
9												
10												
11												
12												
13												
14												
15												
16												
17												
18												
19												
20												
21												
22												
23												
24												
25												
26												
27												
28												
29												
30												
31												

Assign color and mood to a specific square
and color the squares according to
your mood

Mood Tracker

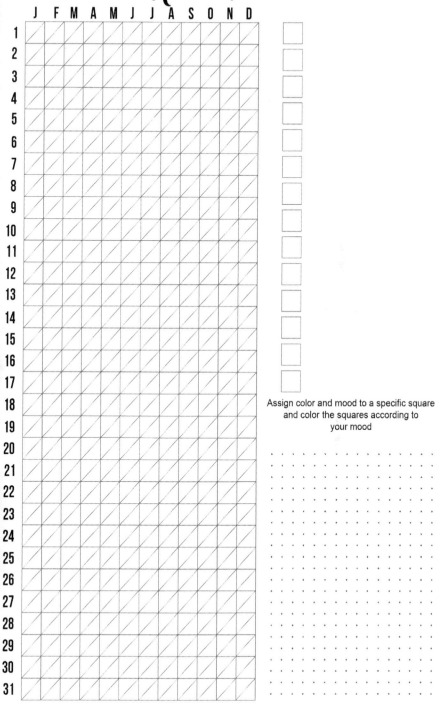

Assign color and mood to a specific square
and color the squares according to
your mood

Mood Tracker

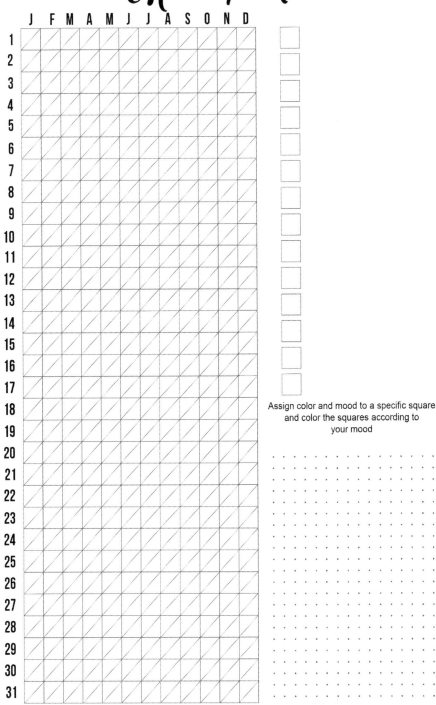

Assign color and mood to a specific square
and color the squares according to
your mood

Mood Tracker

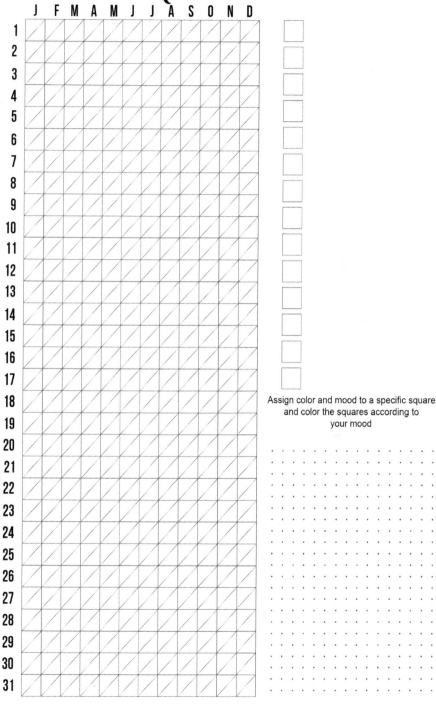

Assign color and mood to a specific square
and color the squares according to
your mood

Mood Tracker

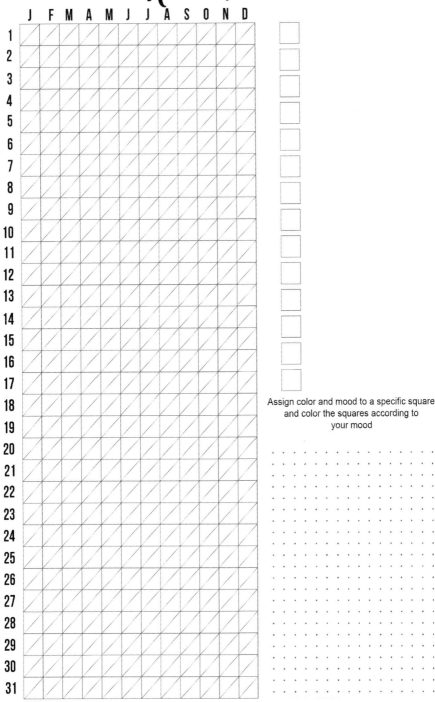

Assign color and mood to a specific square
and color the squares according to
your mood

Mood Tracker

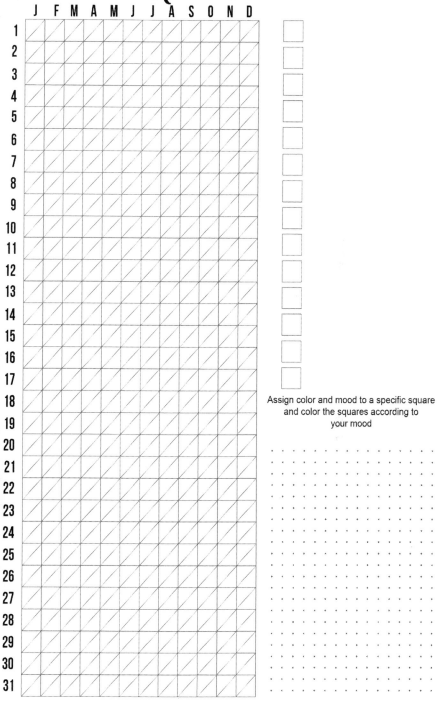

Assign color and mood to a specific square
and color the squares according to
your mood

Mood Tracker

	J	F	M	A	M	J	J	A	S	O	N	D
1												
2												
3												
4												
5												
6												
7												
8												
9												
10												
11												
12												
13												
14												
15												
16												
17												
18												
19												
20												
21												
22												
23												
24												
25												
26												
27												
28												
29												
30												
31												

Assign color and mood to a specific square
and color the squares according to
your mood

Mood Tracker

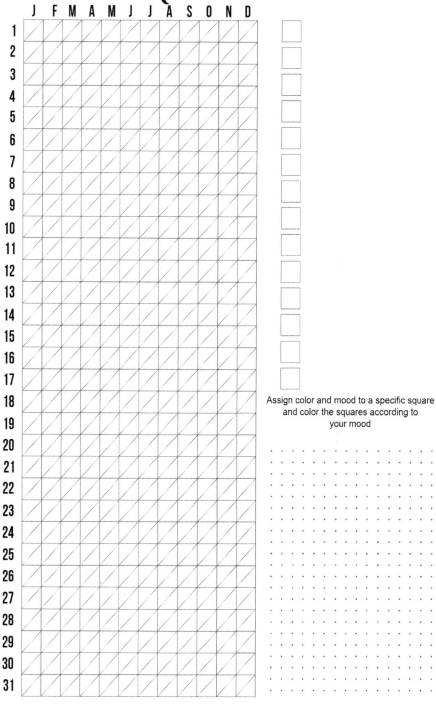

Assign color and mood to a specific square
and color the squares according to
your mood

Made in the USA
Monee, IL
20 November 2024

70669151R00063